PEG'S PET

SHORT E WORDS
Word Preview

hen
pet
set
fed
met
vet
wet
yet
begs
leg
egg
mess
pen
left
yes
let
best
help
nest
Fred
checks

SIGHT-WORDS
Word Preview

gets
red
ten
has
a
is
to
go
and
said
can
you
I
are
will
see
in
an
play
at
the

PEG'S PET

BOOK 2 SHORT E

By Miranda Burnette

Illustrations by Blueberry Illustrations

Keys to Success Publishing, LLC
Atlanta, GA

Copyright © 2016 by Miranda Burnette.

All rights reserved. Published by Keys to Success Publishing, LLC. No part of this book may be reproduced or transmitted in any form or by any means electronic, mechanical, recording, or by any information storage and retrieval system, including photocopying, without permission in writing from the author or publisher.

Printed in the U.S.A.
ISBN – 13: 978-0692925096
ISBN – 10: 0692925090

Keys to Success Publishing
Atlanta, GA

This book is dedicated to my granddaughters, Kyla and Maya. The two girls in this book remind me so much of you, Kyla and Maya. You are both very responsible, helpful and kind. You have the kind of character that will not only take you to great places, but will keep you there. I am so proud of both of you. Keep reaching for the stars and realize your dreams!

Peg has a pet.
The pet is a dog.
Ben is Peg's pet.

Ben makes a mess. The mat gets wet. Ben gets fed.

Peg and Meg are set.
"You are the best," said Peg.

Ben will go to the vet.
The vet is Mr. Fred.
The vet checks
Ben's leg.
Ben's leg is O.K.

Peg, Meg, and Ben left the vet.

"I see a red hen,"
said Peg.
The hen is in a pen.
"I see an egg,"
said Meg.
The egg is in a nest.

Meg and Peg met Jen. Jen is ten. Jen pets Ben.

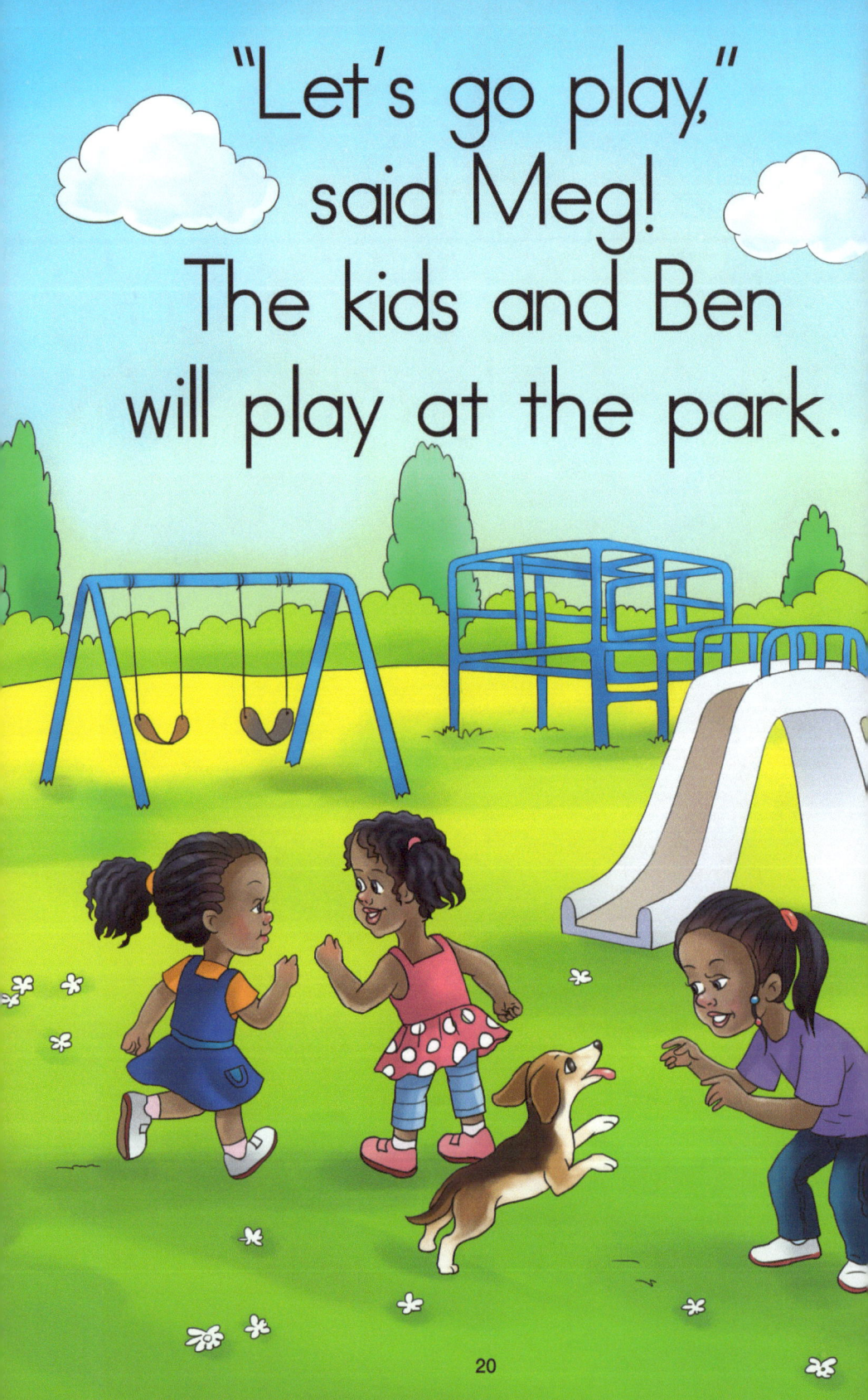
"Let's go play," said Meg! The kids and Ben will play at the park.

READING ACTIVITIES

1. What are the girls' names in the story?

2. Peg and Meg are _____.

3. Where did Peg, Meg and Ben go?

4. Name five words with the *short e* sound.

5. Use the word *Ben* in a sentence.

Miranda Burnette is the president and founder of Miranda Burnette Ministries, Inc., I Can Christian Academy, Inc., and Keys to Success Publishing, LLC.

She is the author of the following books: *Dare to Dream and Soar Like an Eagle*, *Success Starts in Your Mind*, *Leader to Leader*, *Winning With the Power of Love*, and two children books, *Baseball Pals* and *Max and Sam*.

Miranda is passionate about teaching. Prior to resigning and starting her own business, I Can Christian Academy, Inc. in 2009, she taught elementary school for 13 years in the public school system. She has taught several different grade levels but enjoys teaching kindergarten students. Her favorite subject to teach is reading, and she especially loves teaching preschoolers and kindergarten students how to read, as well as teaching young students how to write.

Miranda loves writing inspirational and children's books, reading, and spending time with her grandchildren.

www.ingramcontent.com/pod-product-compliance
Lightning Source LLC
Chambersburg PA
CBHW041810040426
42449CB00001B/52